LOOKING AT LITERATURE

MY FIRST LOOK AT MYTHS

BY ROSIE BANKS

Gareth Stevens PUBLISHING

Please visit our website, www.garethstevens.com. For a free color catalog of all our high-quality books, call toll free 1-800-542-2595 or fax 1-877-542-2596.

Library of Congress Cataloging-in-Publication Data
Names: Banks, Rosie, 1978- author.
Title: My first look at myths / Rosie Banks.
Description: New York : Gareth Stevens Publishing, 2022. | Series: Looking at literature | Includes index.
Identifiers: LCCN 2020028213 (print) | LCCN 2020028214 (ebook) | ISBN 9781538264034 (library binding) | ISBN 9781538264010 (paperback) | ISBN 9781538264027 (6 pack) | ISBN 9781538264041 (ebook)
Subjects: LCSH: Myth–History and criticism–Juvenile literature.
Classification: LCC PN56.M94 B36 2022 (print) | LCC PN56.M94 (ebook) | DDC 398.2–dc23
LC record available at https://lccn.loc.gov/2020028213
LC ebook record available at https://lccn.loc.gov/2020028214

Published in 2022 by
Gareth Stevens Publishing
111 East 14th Street, Suite 349
New York, NY 10003

Designer: Rachel Rising
Editor: Kate Mikoley

Photo credits: Cover, p.1 Larissa Kulik/Shutterstock.com; pp. 3, 4, 6, 8, 10, 12, 14, 16, 18, 20, 21, 22, 23, 24 (background) carduus/ DigitalVision Vectors/Getty Images; p. 5 deliormanli/E+/Getty Images; p. 7 Randy Faris/ The Image Bank/Getty Images; pp. 9, 11, 20 Werner Forman/Universal Images Group/Getty Images; p. 13 Print Collector/Hulton Archive/Getty Images; p. 15 Heritage Images/Hulton Fine Art Collection/Getty Images; p. 17 Image by Adam Young/Moment/Getty Images; p.19 ullstein bild/Contributor/Getty Images; p. 21 Isabella Antonelli/EyeEm/Getty Images.

Printed in the United States of America

CPSIA compliance information: Batch #CSGS22: For further information contact Gareth Stevens, New York, New York at 1-800-542-2595

CONTENTS

Tell Me Why 4
Myths Matter 6
Creation 8
Natural Events 10
Explaining Evil 12
Hero Myths 14
Mythical Rulers 16
Mythical Creatures 18
Read More Myths! 20
Your Turn!. 21
Glossary 22
For More Information 23
Index 24

Boldface words appear in the glossary.

Tell Me Why

People have always had questions about nature. Before they knew about science, they explained the world with stories called myths. For example, the ancient Greeks explained the sun's movement. They said a god pulled the sun across the sky with his **chariot**!

Myths Matter

Every **culture** on Earth has its own myths. Even before people had written language, they were telling each other myths. These stories were told to many, many **generations**. They were how the values and beliefs of a culture were passed on.

Creation

Different cultures have myths about how Earth was **created**. Many myths tell of how a god or gods created the world. One of the creator gods of the Maya people of Mexico and Central America was named Itzamná (eets-ahm-NAH).

Itzamná

Natural Events

Many myths explain natural events. Bali is an island in Southeast Asia. A Balinese myth says the world is on a turtle's back. It's kept there by two serpents, or snakes. When the serpents let go of the world, an **earthquake** happens.

Explaining Evil

Some myths explain why there is evil, or badness, in the world. In Greek myths, a woman named Pandora was told not to open a jar. However, she didn't listen. She opened it and let out the world's evil. In later tellings, the object she opened was a box.

Hero Myths

The ancient Romans borrowed many myths from the Greeks. Aeneas (ih-NEE-uhs) is a hero in Greek and Roman tales. He honored the gods. They helped him found the city of Rome. Heroes like Aeneas taught people how to **behave**.

Aeneas

Mythical Rulers

Some myths are about rulers. The Jade **Emperor** was a figure in Chinese myths. In these tales, he was the ruler of heaven and the first emperor of China. He was kind and fair to his people. Chinese rulers were supposed to behave like him.

Mythical Creatures

You've likely heard of some mythical creatures, like dragons. In African myths, the water spirit Mami Wata looks like a mermaid with a snake. Selkies are in tales from Ireland and Scotland. On land, they look like people. They turn into seals in water!

Mami Wata

Read More Myths!

There are more than 2,000 gods in Egyptian myths! Tales about them hold important clues about an ancient culture. Myths continue to **inspire** artists and writers today.

Discover more about past and present world cultures through their myths!

Your Turn!

Think of a question you have about nature. Use some ideas from this book to make up a myth explaining it. Tell your myth to a friend.

GLOSSARY

behave: to act in a certain way

chariot: a carriage with two wheels that was pulled by horses in ancient times

create: to make something

culture: a group of people with the same beliefs and ways of life

earthquake: a shaking of the ground caused by the movement of Earth's crust

emperor: a man who rules an empire, or a group of countries or regions

generation: a group of people born about the same time

inspire: to cause someone to want to do something

FOR MORE INFORMATION

BOOKS

Chae, Yung In. *Goddess Power: A Kids' Book of Greek and Roman Mythology: 10 Empowering Tales of Legendary Women.* Berkeley, CA: Rockridge Press, 2020.

Fu, Shelley. *Chinese Myths and Legends: The Monkey King and Other Adventures.* Clarendon, VT: Tuttle Publishing, 2018.

WEBSITES

Ancient Egyptian Gods and Goddesses
www.ducksters.com/history/ancient_egyptian_gods_goddesses.php
Discover the famous figures of Egyptian myths.

Children of Odin
www.dltk-kids.com/world/norway/children-of-odin/index.htm
Check out these stories about Norse gods, including Thor.

Myths About the Ancient Greek Gods for Kids
greece.mrdonn.org/myths.html
Read tales about Greek gods, goddesses, and heroes.

Publisher's note to educators and parents: Our editors have carefully reviewed these websites to ensure that they are suitable for students. Many websites change frequently, however, and we cannot guarantee that a site's future contents will continue to meet our high standards of quality and educational value. Be advised that students should be closely supervised whenever they access the Internet.

INDEX

Aeneas 14

Bali 10

China 16

earthquakes 10

gods 4, 8, 14, 20

Greek myths 4, 12, 14

Itzamná 8

Jade Emperor 16

Mami Wata 18

nature 4, 21

Pandora 12

Roman myths 14

Rome 14

selkies 18

sun 4

turtles 10